MW01250772

COCO'S BIRTHDAY
SURPRISE

Angela Sommer-Bodenburg
with illustrations by Agnès Mathieu

Hamish Hamilton - London

A lovely day, a hot, hot sun!
Will Henry's party be much fun?

It was Henry's birthday. Coco had been invited
to his party. The trouble was that she hated her
party clothes! Her red shoes were too tight and
hurt her feet. Her yellow skirt was too tight and
squeezed her tummy. The white blouse which
went with it made her neck itch. The last straw
was an utterly *stupid* straw hat!

"Do I really have to wear all that?" she asked grumpily. "Don't be silly!" said her mother. "Of course you do. Think of all the other crocodile children. They'll all be dressed in their nice party clothes, too."

"Nice?" thought Coco. "Huh! No chance." But the bunch of flowers she had to take to Henry was nice. She got dressed reluctantly and set off.

A lovely day, the sun's warm glow –
Our Coco's progress was quite slow.

She strolled down the High Street,
looking in all the shop windows. There were
brand-new red sports jackets hanging in the
window of the sports shop! She'd love one of
those! In the baker's next door there were
chocolate hippos. Yum! Coco licked her lips at
the thought.

Then she came to a smart shop called Reptile. A
notice read: "Everything for the well-groomed
Crocodile. Foaming bubble bath, dusting
powder, suntan oil, and hair curlers." Yuck!
Coco shuddered. Who wanted to be a well-
groomed crocodile?

Next was the bookshop. Coco loved books, and
gazed at the window longingly. At last she turned
into the lane which ran down to the river.
Henry's house was near the water.

Best make the most of this fine day!
Our Coco dawdled on her way.

There were all kinds of interesting things near
the path. There were ants and spiders, and
beetles running to and fro very busily. There was
a frog sunning himself on a stone, but just as
Coco crept up to him he gave a great leap, and
hopped quickly away. Then she found a snail's
shell. She turned it over, curious to see the snail
inside – but it was empty.

Then she saw a butterfly, resting on a bright
yellow flower. It was the loveliest butterfly Coco
had ever seen! It had wings as blue as the
cornflowers in the meadow, and they were as thin
and fragile as tissue paper.

Quickly Coco took off her shoes, and tiptoed
quietly towards it. But just before she reached
the butterfly, it fluttered away. Backwards and
forwards in the air it flitted before it came down
on another flower. Softly and gently, Coco stole
up to it but just as she was about to stretch out her
hand – it was gone! And there it was, hovering
over a different flower.

Then Coco went quite mad! She chased after the
butterfly as fast as she could run.

Her skirt caught on a bramble, so she pulled it off
and threw it away! Then she threw away her
scratchy blouse.

Last on the grass falls Coco's hat –
No more clothes – just think of that!

Coco spun round in a circle, roaring with
laughter. The grass felt like velvet under her feet.
The green blades softly tickled her legs. The sun
was lovely and warm, and the little breeze
stroked her skin so gently!

Then all of a sudden Coco stopped. She forgot all about chasing the butterfly. She was supposed to be somewhere else!

Coco, the naughty little croc
Remembers Henry – what a shock!

"I shall be too late for the party", she wailed. She grabbed her clothes quickly, and rushed back to the lane.

Oh help! Her straw hat was crushed and dented. Her blouse was all dirty, and there was a hole in her skirt!

And the nice bunch of flowers had wilted. The flower heads drooped as though they were dying of thirst. Coco hadn't even got a proper present for Henry!

A lovely day! A hot, hot sun,
From Coco's eyes big tears did run.

Tears trickled down the little crocodile's cheeks.
She cried and cried, until – all of a sudden – one
of the flowers perked up! Then another, and
another lifted up its head.

The flowers were just as fresh – hooray!
As when she started out today.

Coco waved the flowers in the air. She was
happy! Quickly she pulled on her skirt, stuck her
feet back into her shoes, plonked the straw hat on
her head, and dashed off towards Henry's house.

"I hope no one will laugh at me", she thought. Her heart was pounding as she stood in front of Henry's gate. The birthday party must have started ages ago. She could hear music, and jolly noises. She could smell sausages!

Then Coco saw Henry and the other crocodiles.
They were having a wonderful time running
around in the back garden – and their party
clothes were just as crumpled and dirty as
her own!

Jumping and shouting in the sun –
Yes, Henry's party is great fun!

HAMISH HAMILTON CHILDREN'S BOOKS

Penguin Books Ltd, 27 Wrights Lane, London W8 5TZ (Publishing & Editorial)
and Harmondsworth, Middlesex, England (Distribution & Warehouse)
Viking Penguin Inc., 40 West 23rd Street, New York, New York 10010, U.S.A.
Penguin Books Australia Ltd, Ringwood, Victoria, Australia
Penguin Books Canada Limited, 2801 John Street, Markham, Ontario, Canada L3R 1B4
Penguin Books (N.Z.) Ltd, 182-190 Wairau Road, Auckland 10, New Zealand

First published in Great Britain 1987 by Hamish Hamilton Children's Books

Copyright © 1986 by Otto Maier Verlag Ravensburg
Original German title. «Coco geht zum Geburtstag»

All rights reserved. Without limiting the rights under copyright reserved above, no
part of this publication may be reproduced, stored in or introduced into a retrieval
system, or transmitted, in any form or by any means (electronic, mechanical,
photocopying, recording or otherwise), without the prior written permission of both the
copyright owner and the above publisher of this book.

British Library Cataloguing-in-Publication Data:

Sommer-Bodenburg, Angela
Coco's birthday surprise.
I. Title
833'. 914[J]   PZ7

ISBN 0-241-12301-1

Printed in Italy